Freedom For Real.

15 days of bondage-breaking revelation

Courtney Willie

AF264454

Freedom for real

Copyright © 2024 Courtney Willie

All rights reserved.

ISBN: 978-1-0691171-0-6

Dedication

To Jordan, I wouldn't have done this without you.
To Muriel, I couldn't have done this without you.

Contents

Freedom for real

Introduction:

This 15-day devotional is designed to get you started on your journey through healing, freedom, and faith as you begin to understand the victory that belongs to you, and enforce it over anxiety and depression. Each day aims to bring you closer to God's promises and deeper into His truth. As you work through the reflections, prayers, and challenges, remember that healing is a process, but if you are committed to renewing your mind with God's word, and believing Him over and above every other voice, freedom is not only possible, it's promised.

Day 1: The Lie We've Been Told

Verse: John 8:31-32 (AMP)

So Jesus was saying to the Jews who had believed Him, "If you abide in My word [continually obeying My teachings and living in accordance with them, then] you are truly My disciples. And you will know the truth [regarding salvation], and the truth will set you free [from the penalty of sin]."

Reflection:

I was 13 when someone told me that I was an anorexic and that it was an incurable mental illness that would follow me all of my life, the best I could do was learn to cope. I remember feeling like invisible prison bars were slamming shut all around me. I would NEVER be free of this?

One of the most pervasive lies we've been told is that anxiety and depression are permanent parts of life. Society normalizes these struggles, and we're taught to expect them as inevitable, even unchangeable. But

God's Word tells us something radically different — we have been set free. Whether or not we walk in freedom or bondage is actually up to us.

Now quickly before you throw the book across the room, here's what I am not saying! I am NOT saying that freedom from anxiety and depression is simply a mind over matter discipline. You have been set free, but that doesn't mean that you ARE free. Freedom actually requires a process of identifying wrong beliefs, kicking them out, identifying truth, getting it deep down inside, and then developing a habit of this, along with speaking what God says, rather than what the world says, or even what we feel.

Judging by the sheer volume of air time it gets, mental illness seems to have become the fashion accessory of the season that never ends. We are encouraged to own it, normalize it, and talk about it. Owning it, normalizing it, and talking about it are ways of meditating on it. The more we meditate on something the more we solidify the belief inside our minds that it is true.

But what if we would meditate on and own the new, born-again, holy and righteous identity that Jesus gave us through his death, burial and resurrection? What if we would normalize gratitude for the sound mind he provided? What if we would talk about the life-giving promises, and instructions that God has given us for healthy and wholesome living?

Sickness and fear of any kind are all a part of the penalty of sin, but Romans 6:18 tells us that as believers we have been set free from the penalty of sin. The enemy tries to convince us that anxiety, worry, and fear are too powerful to overcome, but Jesus promises that knowing the truth will liberate us.

The truth is that Jesus came not only to save our souls but to heal our minds. His Word offers real freedom, and it's time to challenge the lies we've accepted for so long. It's time we stopped identifying with what society calls normal, and identify with Christ. We can know the truth, and the truth will set us free.

Prayer:

Lord, reveal the lies I've been believing about my mental health. Guide me to the truth in your Word, and give me eyes that see, ears that hear, and a heart that understands your true nature, and your heart towards me, in Jesus' name, Amen.

Challenge:

Identify one lie you've believed about your mental or emotional struggles. In the reflection above we addressed the lie that mental illness is permanent, and replaced it with the truth that, as disciples of Christ, we will know the truth and the truth sets us free! We have to choose to meditate on that truth until our soul becomes so fully convinced of it that what society calls normal is no longer normal to us, but rather God's truth sets the standard for what's normal in our lives.

Write down the lie the Holy Spirit makes you aware of today and then find a Scripture that speaks truth to it. Meditate on that verse throughout the day.

"ONE OF THE MOST PERVASIVE LIES WE'VE BEEN TOLD IS THAT ANXIETY AND DEPRESSION ARE PERMANENT PARTS OF LIFE."

Day 2: Free to Choose, or Not...

Verse: *Galatians 5:1 (AMP)*

It was for this freedom that Christ set us free [completely liberating us]; therefore keep standing firm and do not be subject again to a yoke of slavery [which you once removed].

Reflection:

It can sometimes feel like mental health struggles are insurmountable, and our thoughts and emotions have us locked in a prison, but let me encourage you, God is in the business of breaking chains, and setting captives free. It's important to know, however, that he will not override our free will. That would be witchcraft.

A part of the freedom Christ died to give us, is the freedom to choose what we will believe, and what we will allow in our lives. Believing truth is not what determines if it's true or not, but it does determine whether or not that truth will impact your life in any way.

God heard the cry of his people who were separated from him by sin in the garden of Eden, so he sent Jesus. Jesus is the healing God provided. Jesus is EVERYTHING we need, the fulfillment of every promise. So what have you done with Jesus? Who is He to you?

It is important that we begin to take responsibility for our relationship with God, Jesus, and the Holy Spirit, or none of this teaching will have any impact. Our prayers remain ineffective if we won't open up the other side of the conversation. You've prayed, but have you asked God for his thoughts on your situation? Have you listened as he explained his ways and his thoughts towards you and for you?

God is not a genie, Jesus is not your enabler, and the Holy Spirit is not your psychedelic experience.

Read that again, it's important that we get that.

Hebrews 4:12-13 (AMPC) says,

12 For the Word that God speaks is alive and full of power [making it active, operative, energizing, and effective]; it is sharper than any two-edged sword, penetrating to the dividing line of the breath of life (soul) and [the immortal] spirit, and of joints and marrow [of the deepest parts of our nature], exposing and sifting and analyzing and judging the very thoughts and purposes of the heart.

13 And not a creature exists that is concealed from His sight, but all things are open and exposed, naked and defenseless to the eyes of Him with Whom we have to do.

It's time to be honest with ourselves about who God really is, who Jesus is, who the Holy Spirit is and whether or not we are giving him the respect, and the position he deserves in our lives. He is a perfect Father, he is a Redeemer, Healer, Restorer, and also the Highest King. Do our lives reflect that we have a perfect Father and King leading, guiding, protecting, teaching, providing for and loving us? There may be some gaps in our relationship, it's time to find them and fill them through intimacy and honor.

Prayer:

Father, I ask for a spirit of wisdom and revelation in the knowledge of you, so that I might receive all that you provided for me through Jesus' death, burial, and resurrection. I trust that You are at work in me, even when I can't see it. I will continue to renew my mind with your word, and believe what you say only, in Jesus' name, Amen.

Challenge:

Spend time meditating on what Jesus accomplished for you today. He endured torture, abuse, fear, abandonment, rejection, any and all of the sicknesses and torments that we can imagine. Now, think on what he accomplished by putting all of those things to death in his body on the cross, defeating Satan and all of his cohorts in hell, then rising to a NEW life, the same life that is available to you NOW. He then sent his same Holy Spirit to live in you! He can't get any closer to you. He is there to teach, guide, comfort, and even pray on your behalf when you don't know how to pray. Spend the most time meditating on the amazing reality of this new life, empowered by his Spirit, that is available to you NOW! Choose today not to let your feelings effect your reality, but rather to agree with the supernatural reality that Jesus provided for you!

> # "GOD IS NOT YOUR GENIE, JESUS IS NOT YOUR ENABLER, AND THE HOLY SPIRIT IS NOT YOUR PSYCHEDELIC EXPERIENCE"

Day 3: The Power of God's Promises

Verse: 2 Corinthians 1:20 (AMPC)

"For as many as are the promises of God, they all find their Yes [answer] in Him [Christ]. For this reason we also utter the Amen (so be it) to God through Him [in His Person and by His agency] to the glory of God."

Reflection:

God's promises are not vague suggestions or empty words, but declarations of his will for us. When it comes to anxiety and depression, God has promised us peace, healing, and wholeness, but these are a gift. Gifts must be received and opened in order to have any impact in our lives.

How do we open up the gifts or promises of God? By faith, we have to take God at his Word. If he says we have the mind of Christ, then we have to choose to believe him! One of the most encouraging aspects of his promises is that they are guaranteed in Christ to all who will believe.

We read in 2 Corinthians 1:22,

22 *[He has also appropriated and acknowledged us as His by] putting His seal upon us and giving us His [Holy] Spirit in our hearts as the security deposit and guarantee [of the fulfillment of His promise].*

He has so much love and faith in us that he has put a security deposit down on our souls. He gave us his very own Spirit, knowing that we are free to reject it, allow it to lie dormant within us, or to open it up and enjoy it for all it's worth.

He has called us his own, and given us access to everything that belongs to him, but it's up to us now to join our faith with his. We have to put in a deposit of faith in order to access the fullness of what's available by the Spirit. Get this though, God's grace, or his empowerment, is so great towards us, that he doesn't even expect us to understand the whole process, or follow 12 steps before we can receive. For God, it' s enough for you to simply say, "God, what do you say about this? I choose to believe you."

Once we have made the decision to believe God, and let his Word be the final authority we have to commit to the process of renewing our minds. We do this by keeping his Word before our eyes, putting it in our ears, and speaking it out loud, declaring that this is what we will believe now over and above anything or anyone else. As we do this we literally begin to alter the physical structure of our brains. We pave new roads in our minds, we bring our will into agreement with God's will, and we harness our emotions so that they are no longer in charge, but merely a gauge.

No matter how impossible it feels to break free from mental or emotional struggles, God's Word says otherwise. Will you choose to believe your feelings, or to believe Almighty God? It's easy to forget or doubt his promises when we feel pain or distress in our bodies and the world offers so many quick fixes, but those fixes are temporary, and always with negative side-effects. God's promises are eternal and life-changing, always producing fruit and overflow. Hebrews 10:23 encourages us,

Let us seize and hold tightly to the confession of our hope without wavering, for He who promised is reliable and trustworthy and faithful [to His word];

It's important to remember that God is faithful to *His* Word, and no one else's. You don't get to declare whatever you want God to do for you and have it done. You can only declare what God has already spoken, and promised to you. His faith and power have already been released towards you through the Words that he has spoken. You receive them by speaking the same thing, and releasing your faith in him and his Word. He is always faithful to come through on your behalf when you will put your faith in him, even above your own natural feelings and reality.

Prayer:

Lord, thank You that Your promises are always "yes" and "amen." Today, Lord, I choose to trust that you are faithful to your Word! Thank you for the spirit you have given me, of power, love, and a sound, disciplined mind, in Jesus' name, Amen.

Challenge:

Choose one promise of God from the Bible that speaks directly to a struggle you're facing. Write it down and place it somewhere visible, like on your mirror or phone. Meditate on that promise throughout the day.

____

____

____

____

____

____

____

____

____

____

____

____

____

____

"...GOD HAS PROMISED US PEACE, HEALING, AND WHOLENESS, BUT THESE ARE A GIFT."

Day 4: Learn from the Old, Live in the New

Verse: Romans 12:2 (NLT)

"Don't copy the behavior and customs of this world, but let God transform you into a new person by changing the way you think. Then you will learn to know God's will for you, which is good and pleasing and perfect."

Reflection:

Our culture often normalizes anxiety, stress, and depression. It's easy to feel trapped in these cycles because everyone around us seems to struggle with the same issues, and even flaunts them like they are merit badges. It appears like the more issues you have, the more true to yourself you are being.

Religion isn't any more helpful, telling us that God has made us sick to teach us a lesson, or to use our lives as a testimony to others. I am going to be bold on this point, because nothing is more disheartening than Christians keeping other Christians in bondage. Those who are ignorant of God's word may not understand truth, and need to be taught, but believers, we have no excuse.

We are New Testament believers because we are living in a new Kingdom reality. We still need the WHOLE Bible, but our reality is different than an old testament believer's. Old Testament believers could not approach God as a child, they relied on animal sacrifice for purification and a priest as a mediator between them and God. We have the Spirit of God literally making his home inside of us. He is available to us at every moment, and he's closer than our own skin.

Jesus paid the price for sickness, sin and death, taking our punishment and the consequences of our sin on himself. If God chose to still punish you for your sins, or let you remain ill as some kind of testimony to others (honestly, what kind of a testimony is that) then he would be stating that Jesus' death, burial, and resurrection weren't enough, and that, my friend, is simply not the case.

Mental illness is not a gift from God. If it was, there is no chance that I would be here, encouraging you to follow a god as twisted, manipulative, and unloving as that.

Jesus took it all for us! That's the gospel! That God loved us so much he sent his son to bridge the gap, pay for sin, provide for every spiritual, physical, mental and emotional need, and to restore us to unity with him. You and I no longer have to carry the weight of punishment or shame! Rather the word tells us,

He personally bore our sins in His [own] body on the tree [as on an altar and offered Himself on it], that we might die (cease to exist) to sin and live to righteousness. By His wounds you have been healed. - 1 Peter 2:24 (AMPC)

In Christ, we have also died to sin and sickness, and have been raised to NEW life, empowered and filled with his Spirit!

That means the only way that sickness is allowed to operate inside of our born again person is if we LET IT! Meditate on that for a minute. Your faith in Jesus is so powerful! What God has spoken set everything into motion. When you choose to believe what God has said you are releasing faith, and allowing God's Word to operate in your life. When you do not believe God's Word above any other word, or when you are ignorant of what God's Word says, its ability to operate in your life is limited. God's normal is so different, and he is calling us higher.

He tells us not to conform to the world's way of thinking but to be transformed by the renewing of our minds. This transformation comes through immersing ourselves in Scripture, allowing God's truth to replace the lies of the world, and even the lies that we have been taught by religion.

It is in this renewal that we begin to experience freedom and healing. It's abandonding an old way of thinking to adopt a brand new one. This doesn't happen by default, it requires intentionality on our part. Mainly, it's about deepening your intimacy with God himself. As we begin to truly know him everything else begins to line up.

Prayer:

Father, help me not to conform to the patterns of this world, but instead renew my mind with Your truth. Let me see my life and struggles through Your eyes, and not through the lens of the culture around me, in Jesus' name, Amen.

Challenge:

Take a moment to reflect on how cultural expectations, or religious teachings have influenced your thoughts about mental illness, anxiety or depression. Ask God to help you see where you've conformed to the world, and ask for his help in renewing your mind.

"MENTAL ILLNESS IS NOT A GIFT FROM GOD."

Day 5: The Choice to Believe

Verse: Mark 9:23 (CSB)

"Everything is possible for the one who believes."

Reflection:

One of the most important steps in our healing journey is choosing to believe God's promises. Doubt is natural, but faith is a choice. Jesus tells us that everything is possible for those who believe. When we choose to believe God's Word over our circumstances, we open the door for miracles and healing to take place in our lives.

Our belief activates God's power in ways we can't fully understand. That's important to hear. You don't have to understand how a miracle or healing will work in order for it to work, but you do have to believe that it will work. Surrender your ideas for how you think it should be done, and ask the Lord for the vision.

Habakkuk 2:2 says, *"Then the Lord answered me and said, "Write the vision and engrave it plainly on [clay] tablets so that the one who reads it will run."*

God created us with imaginations so that we can see and picture something long before we hold it in our hands. That is why he tells us to write the vision plainly, and put it where we will see it continually so that it will become engraved on the inside of us, and we will begin to see it with our spiritual eyes, and attain it by faith, or by believing that we have it. What you can believe you can behold.

There was a time in my life when I faced an overwhelming situation that completely overpowered my natural strength, and understanding. I was so completely blindsided that I didn't even know how to think or feel, but the negative pressure threatened to crush me. In that moment all I knew to do was keep my mouth shut, and turn to my Heavenly Father.

I asked the Lord to give me a word, and began to pray in tongues, and worship. Singing praise, and giving thanks are not easy when the breath has been squeezed from your lungs, but I knew that this situation was so far beyond the help of any natural solution, or person. Only God could help me here, so I would thank him for being enough, even for this.

For 3 days I had to resist fear, and bite my tongue, opening it only to pray in tongues and thank the Lord for the answer he would bring, and he did bring an answer. I didn't receive an instant miracle, but I received a promise, and a word from the Lord that I could stand on.

Guess what, it took years to see the full manifestation of that promise. There were many doubts and fears that tried to take root during that time, but I continued to speak the same word the Lord had given me. It's important that we do this. Rather than constantly seeking a new word, or a new earth-shattering, goosebump inducing experience, we need to stand on the last thing he said, walking in obedience until the thing is done.

It didn't take years for the full manifestation because God was holding out on me. It took years, because that's how long it took to develop my faith to receive the fullness of the promise. It was a big problem, with a God-sized solution. For some of us, it takes time to renew our minds, resist worldly input, and to get to know the heart of our loving Heavenly Father.

Guess what else? It was worth the wait! Don't give up on what God speaks to you. Don't believe, or even entertain the thought, "It didn't work," "I'm too far gone," or "It came back, maybe this won't work for me."

Ephesians 6:13-14 says, *"For this reason take up the full armor of God, so that you may be able to resist in the evil day, and having prepared everything, to take your stand."*

Prepare by putting on the full armor (found in the rest of Ephesians 6), resist the devil, and STAND!

Prayer:

Lord God, help me overcome my unbelief. I choose to believe in Your promises today. Help my unbelief, and help me trust You, even when it's difficult, in Jesus' name, Amen.

Challenge:

Write a declaration of faith today. Start with the words, "I choose to believe..." and fill in the blanks with God's promises that speak to your struggles.

____

____

____

____

____

____

____

____

____

____

____

____

____

____

____

____

"WE NEED TO STAND ON THE LAST THING HE SAID, WALKING IN OBEDIENCE UNTIL THE THING IS DONE."

Day 6: Numb From the Roots Up

Verse: 1 Peter 5:6-7 (AMP)

Humble yourselves, therefore, under the mighty hand of God, so that he may exalt you at the proper time, casting all your cares on him, because he cares about you.

Reflection:

Coping mechanisms, whether in the form of medication, distractions, or unhealthy habits, can often numb us to the root issues we need to address. When we numb ourselves, we may escape pain, but we also lose the ability to experience true peace, joy, and freedom.

Maybe it's the zombie-like scrolling on your phone, or turning on the tv as soon as you get home, or maybe it's substance abuse, or retail-therapy. Whatever your drug of choice, it's keeping you trapped. Rather then helping you to heal past your hurts, it keeps you stuck in a constant state of trying to forget, trying to drown out the voices or avoid feeling pain.

What would happen if you could muster up the courage to face the fear and the pain once and for all? What if I told you that you don't even have to find the strength to do that in yourself, but that God himself will face down whatever it is that is tormenting you, and together, you and your Heavenly Father could turn the tides of your damaging cycles, turning them into a journey to wholeness? Would you dare to trust him?

God invites us to cast all our anxiety on him because he cares deeply for us. He doesn't offer temporary fixes — he offers complete healing and restoration. Trusting him fully means letting go of the things we use to cope and allowing his grace to transform us from the inside out. It also means, allowing him to take us by the hand and walk us THROUGH the valley of the shadow of death aka, face the fears that have kept you imprisoned, and recognize them for the powerless lies that they are. No more avoiding them, but also, no more being tormented by them.

I do NOT think it's helpful to meditate on wrongs done, abuses endured, and traumas experienced, as some therapies encourage. Nowhere in scripture does the Lord lead us to dig deep to discover which parent is to blame for every irrational fear and phobia in our lives. He does tell us to cast our cares on him, and that requires intentional focus and action.

What we do find in scripture is the reminder not to let shame and fear have power over our lives (Romans 8:1), and to take responsibility for our own souls (Phillipians 2:12). This means you will have to ask the Holy Spirit to show you wrong thought patterns, that may have developed out of old hurts that did not heal.

When we allow the Holy Spirit to flip on the lights in all the dark corners of our being, we discover quickly that those demons who are making big scary noises are actually weasely little wimps, and the shame that has entangled us is nothing more than noodle chains.

We don't need to dwell on the negative pieces of the past, but we do need to bring them out into the light so the Lord can transform how we see them, and bring complete healing to the old wounds.

Prayer:

Heavenly Father, I surrender the things I've been using to cope with my anxiety and depression. I don't want to be numb — I want to be healed. Show me how to cast my cares on You and find true freedom in Your love, in Jesus' name, Amen.

Challenge:

Take inventory of the ways you've been coping with your anxiety or depression. What are you using to numb yourself? Write them down and pray over them, asking God to help you let go and rely on him. Then invite the Holy Spirit to search out the dark corners and show you what things you've been avoiding that are behaving like infected wounds in your soul.

> "HE DOESN'T OFFER TEMPORARY FIXES — HE OFFERS COMPLETE HEALING AND RESTORATION."

Day 7: The Role of the Holy Spirit in Healing

Verse: John 14:26 (CSB)

"But the Counselor, the Holy Spirit, whom the Father will send in my name, will teach you all things and will remind you of everything I have told you."

Reflection:

The Holy Spirit is our Counselor, Advocate, and Helper. When it comes to healing from anxiety and depression, the Holy Spirit plays a vital role in guiding us through the process. The Holy Spirit knows every detail of our hearts and minds, and he can lead us to the truth we need to experience freedom. He's not just a passive presence — He actively teaches, reminds, and comforts us as we walk out this journey.

It's so easy to lose touch with our souls in the busyness of our modern lives. Not only are our schedules full, but we are being bombarded with images, content, advertising, agendas, and unfiltered opinions, and it can muddy our own thinking and deciphering. The Holy Spirit is there to help us discern truth from someone else's bitter venting, and also to give us a nudge when our own soul is out of balance.

I can't even count how many times I thought "I'm fine" right before spiraling into a full nervous breakdown. Even still, I have to be very intentional at making the time and space to ask the Holy Spirit to give me a check-up. It has to be him that leads the check-up, because if it's me, I can let my thoughts or feelings tell me one thing, or old self-preservation tactics step in to tell me "I'm fine, bury it deep and grind on!"

At this point in my relationship with the Holy Spirit, I pray every time I read my Bible that he would teach me what I'm reading, and he regularly stops me. He will tell me to go back and reread something again, and again, and again, and usually around the fifth time the lightbulb comes on and he downloads a whole new revelation to me about a scripture I have read thousands of times before. Through that scripture he will reveal something in me that needs realigning. These are always welcome and beautiful experiences, never condemning or icky.

Developing a relationship with the Holy Spirit means inviting him into our daily lives, and giving him permission to interrupt us in order to teach and train us. When we don't know how to pray, he can pray on our behalf, using the language of Heaven to communicate with God himself. There is no separation between us and God when we have the Holy Spirit living inside of us. We can trust his leading.

If you have never prayed in tongues, I encourage you to invite the Holy Spirit to fill you up with himself, then open your mouth and yield to him. It may sound ridiculous, don't judge it. Let it be what it is, supernatural, not natural. We are to continually make a habit of being filled with the Spirit, so that we continually have the grace that empowers us for every task, and keeps us under His divine protection and blessing.

Prayer:

God, I ask that you give me the gift of your Holy Spirit, I invite you, Holy Spirit now to fill me up. Lead me into truth and guide me on the path to healing. I trust You to be my Counselor, Helper, and Advocate as I walk out this journey, in Jesus' name, Amen.

Challenge:

Spend time today praying in tongues, allowing your inner man to be strengthened as you do so. Ask the Holy Spirit to guide you and speak to you as you open your heart to his leading. Write down what he speaks to you.

"THERE IS NO SEPARATION BETWEEN US AND GOD WHEN WE HAVE THE HOLY SPIRIT LIVING INSIDE OF US."

Day 8: God's Word is Alive and Active

Verse: Hebrews 4:12 (CSB)

"For the word of God is living and effective and sharper than any double-edged sword, penetrating as far as the separation of soul and spirit, joints and marrow. It is able to judge the thoughts and intentions of the heart."

Reflection:

God's Word is not just a historical document or a book of rules. John 1:1 tells us,

"In the beginning there was the Word. The Word was with God, and the Word was God."

The Word WAS God Himself. The Word is alive and powerful, capable of transforming our hearts and minds. When we immerse ourselves in Scripture, we are inviting God's healing presence into our lives. We are aligning our thoughts with his thoughts and our words with his Words. This is where the power is.

His Word cuts through the lies, the doubts, and the anxieties that hold us captive. As we renew our minds with God's word we align ourselves with God's will for our lives and we are actually transformed (Romans 12:2). The more we meditate on his Word, the more we begin to experience the freedom and peace that come from knowing his truth.

I got saved as a child, but I didn't experience anything I would describe as transformative, in the area of my thoughts and emotions, until I decided to go all-in for Jesus and his word as a 20-year-old. I committed then to actively replace wrong thinking with the Word of God.

It's a process, and it takes very intentional action on our part. We don't have to work to earn God's promises, they already belong to us, but we do have to work to unlearn the things that have kept us bound in doubt, fear and unbelief. We are responsible for actively replacing those lies with the truth. As we do so, the truth begins to cut out the gunk in our souls, exposing what else needs to be removed and restored.

Second Corinthians 10:5 says *"We are destroying sophisticated arguments and every exalted and proud thing that sets itself up against the [true] knowledge of God, and we are taking every thought and purpose captive to the obedience of Christ,"*

You and I have to actively take captive every wrong thought, and exchange it for the truth of God's word, until the lies become less and less, and the truth is the prevailing message within our thoughts and lives.

So, how do we know what's a lie and what's the truth, when the world is so loud around us, and the church can be so divided amongst itself? This brings us back to yesterdays reading. We have been given the gift of God's own Spirit, living inside of us, to teach us to discern truth from a lie. Ask the Holy Spirit regularly to guide and direct your steps, to point out anything in you that is not in alignment with your God-given identity, and pray in tongues to build up your spiritual muscle.

The Holy Spirit always leads us through His Word. God has laid out His plans and purposes for us in his Word, and the more familiar we are with the voice of our Heavenly Father the more obvious all other lying voices become. The more time we spend in his presence the more we are aware when we begin to be separated by wrong thinking.

By his Spirit and his Word we can begin to discern lie from truth, worldly reason and logic from godly identity and authority.

Prayer:

Lord, thank You for the power of Your Word. I ask that You would make it alive in my heart and mind today. Let it penetrate the areas of my life that need healing and bring transformation, in Jesus' name, Amen.

Challenge:

Today, practice thinking about your thoughts. Take an inventory. What do you think about most? What is the overall attitude or tone of most of your thoughts? Find a scripture that addresses these things and meditate on it today, asking God to make his Word come alive in your heart and mind.

> "BY HIS SPIRIT AND HIS WORD WE CAN BEGIN TO DISCERN LIE FROM TRUTH,"

Day 9: Overcoming Fear

Verse: 2 Timothy 1:7 (NKJV)

"For God has not given us a spirit of fear, but of power and of love and of a sound mind."

Reflection:

Fear is one of the root causes of anxiety and depression. Fear of the unknown, fear of failure, fear of the future — these fears keep us trapped in cycles of worry and despair. But God has not given us a spirit of fear. His Spirit brings power, love and a sound mind.

When we align ourselves with God's truth, and allow the Holy Spirit to fill us up, we can enforce our victory over fear. Fear no longer has to control us, because we serve a God who is greater than anything we face. When we get a revelation of this we can laugh in the face of fear, in chaos we can keep our peace, and we can have joy, even in the most desparate, disparaging moments, because we know and are convinced that through it all God is with us, he is for us, and this will end victoriously.

If you knew you were going to win every race you ran, how many races would you bow out of for fear of failing? NONE! The same is true of our race as believers. We win! So keep running, and don't let the distractions of life pull you out of your lane. Fix your eyes on Jesus, and finish your race.

Resisting fear might sound like some far-off hyper-spiritual concept, but can I make it practical for you? When a thought comes that smells like fear, tastes like fear, or causes your inner man to tremble with fear, stop it in it's tracks! Speak out loud, say "No, I will not think that thought. Fear, I resist you in the Name of Jesus!" Then exercise self-discipline and choose what you will think instead.

If the fear is surrounding a certain problem or challenging circumstance, spend some time praying in tongues and ask the Holy Spirit to give you a word on the matter. DO NOT DWELL ON THE TROUBLING THOUGHT OR EXPERIENCE. Instead dwell on the goodness and faithfulness of God.

Push fear away like a scammy telemarketer, say a firm "No sirree!" then hang up the phone! Then press in for a time of intimacy with your Father. When the Lord gives you a word (that will always be found IN his Word), you speak it boldly, declaring, "I will not believe that lie, because I choose to believe what my Heavenly Father says, which is...."

Then refuse to get back on the negative, fearful thought train. Don't even turn back to wave goodbye, just move forward, headlong into grace and truth. This takes practice. It can be hard not to pick up the care again and again, or to let those thoughts circle around and around, but continue to push them away.

Choose what you will think on. Philippians 4:8 in the Amplified Bible says, *"Finally, believers, whatever is true, whatever is honorable and worthy of respect, whatever is right and confirmed by God's word, whatever is pure and wholesome, whatever is lovely and brings peace, whatever is admirable and of good repute; if there is any excellence, if there is anything worthy of praise, think continually on these things [center your mind on them, and implant them in your heart]."*

The Lord is working out the answer in you, and as you continue to spend time praying in tongues, and being still in his presence, learning to listen with your spiritual ears, he will reveal your next steps to you. However, you will only be able to hear clearly when your mind is not muddled with the crazed voices of fear. Be on guard! Silence fear continually, and make space to be with God. That's where all the answers are waiting for you, as soon as you have the capacity to hear.

Prayer:

Lord, I surrender my fears to You today. I know You have not given me a spirit of fear, but of power and love and a sound mind. Help me walk in that truth, trusting You to lead me through every challenge, in Jesus' name, Amen.

Challenge:

Identify one fear that has been holding you back. Write it down and ask the Holy Spirit to reveal the root to you, as well as a scripture that you can meditate on to dismantle this lie.

____

____

____

____

____

____

____

____

____

____

____

____

____

____

____

"FIX YOUR EYES ON JESUS, AND FINISH YOUR RACE."

Day 10: What Do You Think?

Verse: Philippians 4:8 (NLT)

"Fix your thoughts on what is true, and honorable, and right, and pure, and lovely, and admirable. Think about things that are excellent and worthy of praise."

Reflection:

The Bible teaches us that what we think about shapes our reality. Our minds are powerful, and the thoughts we dwell on can either lead us toward freedom or keep us in bondage. Anxiety and depression often take root in our minds through negative, destructive thought patterns, but God calls us to think about what is true, noble, and right.

For most of my life I thought that my feelings were the gauge for how I was doing, and how my life was going. I also didn't know that I didn't actually have to think on every thought that arose in my mind. How I felt about something is what made it good or bad. If I felt depressed, I was depressed, and would be until someting made me happy again. Maybe this is your first time hearing this, like it was mine as a young adult, but you don't have to think about every thought you have, nor do you have to feel every emotion that arises.

When we intentionally fill our minds with God's truth, we begin to experience a transformation in the way we think and feel. This is a process. Consider how long your thinking has been running wild with no discipline, no boundaries, and no filter? It's going to take some time to reign in those rebel thoughts, and even after you've kicked them out, they will try to climb back in a window that you left open. Keep at it! Don't give up.

Remember, that you have to SPEAK to your thoughts. You can't outthink a thought, you have to speak to it. Declare the word of God over your mind, over your body, over your thoughts, and be intentional about which thought-trains you jump on and which ones you let go whistling by.

As we begin to practice self-discipline in our thoughts and feelings, the Holy Spirit is able to teach us to discern which ones are signs of a deeper issue, and which ones are attacks from the enemy and need to be completely rejected. Regardless, you never have to dwell on the negative thoughts and emotions, but you do have to talk to them, and exercise your authority over them. Remind them that you are the boss, and as the boss, you have put the Holy Spirit in charge of thought and emotion quality control, not Fear, Depression, or Self-doubt. Those losers are fired.

Yesterday we learned how to resist fear, but now what do we do with a thought or an emotion that sticks around like an unwanted relative? Well, for starters, put a lock on the fridge, and make a note not to open the door next time. Then, you have to bring it before the throne.

Carry that thought, emotion, problem, worry, relationship, whatever it is, before your Father and King. Lay it down at his feet. Be bold in declaring that you trust him to handle it, and give thanks to him for the way that he loves and cares for you! Now turn and leave the room, leaving the problem at the feet of God Almighty. He's got this.

Don't go back to pick up your care! Ask the Holy Spirit for the next step, and be quick to listen and obey.

"And we know [with great confidence] that God [who is deeply concerned about us] causes all things to work together [as a plan] for good for those who love God, to those who are called according to His plan and purpose."
- Romans 8:28 (AMP)

Prayer:

Father, I ask for Your help in renewing my mind. Help me focus on what is true and good, rather than the negative thoughts that often consume me. Guide me in replacing lies with Your truth, in Jesus' name, Amen.

Challenge:

Write down any recurring negative thoughts you've been struggling with. Then, find a Scripture that speaks truth to each one. Meditate on those Scriptures throughout the day.

"YOU CAN'T OUTTHINK A THOUGHT, YOU HAVE TO SPEAK TO IT."

Day 11: Trusting God More Than Medicine

Verse: Psalm 118:8 (CSB)

"It is better to take refuge in the Lord than to trust in humanity."

Reflection:

At 18 years old I spiraled into the worst depression I had faced yet. Not knowing where to turn I ended up in a doctor's office. The doctor told me that I was chemically imbalanced, and would need to rely on medication to function normally.

It was yet another life-shaping lie that I believed. So I went on the medication. What followed was not freedom. In fact the only word that can describe my experience is "numbing." I felt nothing, I had no opinions, or thoughts, and the music and poetry that I used to write had completely dried up. I became a zombie.

This experience just fed the lie that life was a hopeless, miserable struggle and I would just have to keep coping to get by. That is until I began to hear the Word in a way I had never heard it before. I began to hear teaching about God's Word being life and health to our whole bodies, and the people that were sharing this news spoke about the Word as though it was perfectly relevant and applicable to their lives.

I wanted what they had!

I wanted to be able to apply the truths of God's Word to my life in the same way that they were doing and I wanted the results they were getting, namely joy and peace. Finally, I had had enough of depression and anxiety and I decided to put it all on the line for Jesus.

I decided that the Word of God would be my medicine. I AM NOT telling ANYONE to throw away their medication, but that is the way the Lord led me. The important part is that we begin to make God's word a higher authority, higher than any other words that have been spoken. As we submit to the leading of the Holy Spirit he will reveal the plan for each step of our individual journey.

I want to be very, very clear on this. Medicine is not the enemy of faith! If you are currently medicated, or you feel led by the Holy Spirit to go on medication there is NO condemnation.

"Therefore, there is now no condemnation for those in Christ Jesus, because the law of the Spirit of life in Christ Jesus has set you free from the law of sin and death."- Romans 8:1-2 (CSB)

Medicine can be a helpful tool in our journey to healing, but it is not the ultimate solution. OTC medications have become so culturally acceptable that we don't even question them anymore. I am simply asking you to question them before choosing to put the whole weight of your health and faith upon them. What does the Lord have to say to you about medicine? Whether it be antidepressants or Tylenol, what is the Lord saying?

We are instructed to remain sober-minded (1 Peter 5:8) and if that's the instruction the Lord gives, then he has also supplied everything we need in order to do so. God will never ask us to do something that he will not empower us to do. He does ask us to do things that we cannot do apart from his Spirit.

"'Not by strength or by might, but by my Spirit,' says the LORD *of Armies."- Zechariah 4:6 (CSB)*

It's easy to accept medication or other coping mechanisms that have become so familiar to us, as fine, or even good, but have we taken the time to ask God, the ultimate Healer, for his thoughts. Trusting God doesn't mean we reject medical help altogether, but it does mean that our primary faith should be in his power to heal us — spirit, mind, and body. It means, taking the time to ask him first, to trust him the most.

It's easy to say that you believe that God is willing and able to heal you, but it's another thing entirely to believe that he HAS healed you. Until you have allowed the Holy Spirit to teach and reveal that truth to you, you will not experience it in your natural life. God will not make you receive the blessings he has provided.

Before you can hold the full manifestation of God's promise in your hands, you must fully rely on and trust that what he said is true.

We have to be honest with ourselves about what we really have the faith to believe for. If all you have the faith to believe for is that medication will help, then start there, but ask the Lord to reveal his plan for your healing journey, and begin to stretch your faith. I have found that when I allowed God to speak a word concerning my situation and then I determine to believe and act on what he has said, his grace fills the gap where I don't fully have what I need yet.

I may not be fully convinced that I have it yet, but if I determine that I WILL hold it because he said I would, and he is teaching me how, then his grace will empower me for the journey.

God is our refuge, and he alone knows the full extent of our needs. The thing about western medicine, and all worldly coping mechanisms is that they all carry with them some form of side-effect, plus they are never a permanent fix.

The only way to live out a life of freedom is to allow the Author of Freedom itself to lead you through the story of your life. He will reveal to you the right path at the right time. He has always provided a perfect, and permanent solution for everything we might face, and it's our responsibility to turn ourselves over to him for teaching, guidance, and revelation.

God doesn't want you to stay sick, nor does he want you to live numb and medicated. He wants you to walk in the FULLNESS of the healing, redemption, restoration, and freedom that he has made available to all who will renew their minds, and commit to the transformative journey of believing and being in relationship with Him.

God desires that you would trust him more than anything or anyone else, so that he can overwhelm you with his love and abundant provision for your every need.

Prayer:

Lord, help me to trust You above all else. I will seek you for wisdom every step of the way, and I thank You for leading me. I place my faith in You as my Healer. Show me how to rely on You more fully each day, in Jesus' name, Amen.

Challenge:

Reflect on areas of your life where you might be placing more trust in human solutions (like medication or advice) than in God. Write down a prayer asking God to help you trust Him above all.

____

____

____

____

____

____

____

____

____

____

____

____

____

____

____

"WE HAVE TO BE HONEST WITH OURSELVES ABOUT WHAT WE REALLY HAVE THE FAITH TO BELIEVE FOR."

Day 12: Enforcing Victory Over Fear

Verse: Isaiah 41:10 (CSB)

"Do not fear, for I am with you; do not be afraid, for I am your God. I will strengthen you; I will help you; I will hold on to you with my righteous right hand."

Reflection:

The fear of failure is one of the most paralyzing fears we can face. It prevents us from stepping out in faith, from trying new things and from trusting God fully. For much of my life, the fear of failure kept me paralyzed. I would rather do nothing at all than do something poorly or wrong.

If we really dig to the bottom of this fear we will discover that it's rooted in a fear of man. We want people to like us, to approve of us, to be proud of us. The fear of being rejected keeps us from beginning relationships, or fighting for them when things get tough.

For some of you this fear may stem from actual trauma or abuse. Maybe it was those closest to you, who you should have been able to trust, who rejected you or abandoned you or made you feel like you were never enough.

Often we operate in the fear of man disguised as self-preservation. Our fears are the only way that we know how to protect ourselves from pain.

God's Word has good news for us. He reassures us that we don't need to fear. In fact he tells us that fear has nothing to do with God. 1 John 4:18 tells us that perfect love (which is God Himself) casts out fear. So anxiety, or the fear of failure, or the fear of people, or pain itself, is not from him and he has empowered us to cast it out.

No matter what fear we face, his grace is sufficient. His grace is more than enough to make anxiety irrelevant. Even if we stumble, he will catch us. Even if we experience pain, he will turn it for our good, and heal all that hurts. There is no kick that will keep you down, because Jesus will have your back. His presence in our lives guarantees that we can move forward with confidence, knowing that he will never leave us nor forsake us.

Like a good parent, God will instruct us in how to live a life of peace, blessing and protection, but also like a good parent, he will allow us to make our own mistakes. There is a different grace on a new believer, or spiritual baby, but ultimately, the Lord will not override our free will. He has given us his Word, and his Spirit, meaning that we don't actually have to walk through a single moment of our lives without help, guidance, protection, blessing, favor, and every other promise of God. However, it's up to you and I to choose how many moments of our day we will actually walk under that covering.

When we choose to make choices that go against God's guidance and instruction, God will not protect us from the consequences. We have stepped out from under his protective umbrella and we are going to feel the rain. All it takes to get back under the umbrella is an acknowledgment and repentance, or turning back. "Sorry Lord, I get it now, you lead, I'll follow," and just like that we are back under the blessing of God.

When anxiety tries to rear it's ugly head, turn to your Heavenly Father and choose to fix your gaze on him and all that he has made available to you, choosing to rest in his strong arms, because he's got you! Take the step in faith, even if it scares you, keeping your eyes on him, letting him lead you through to the other side.

Prayer:

Lord, I give You my fear of failure and fear of what other people think of me, today. Help me step out in faith, trusting that You are with me no matter what. I know that with You, I cannot fail, in Jesus' name, Amen.

Challenge:

Identify one area where fear of failure, fear of people, or any fear has been holding you back. Practice resting in his arms today, trusting that he's got you. Then take a step of faith in one area, maybe you need to take the time to ask him what that looks like, when he shows you, obey quickly, trusting that God is with you.

"HIS GRACE IS MORE THAN ENOUGH TO MAKE ANXIETY IRRELEVANT."

Day 13: Trusting God's Plan

Verse: Jeremiah 29:11 (AMP)

"For I know the plans and thoughts that I have for you,' says the LORD, *'plans for peace and well-being and not for disaster, to give you a future and a hope."*

Reflection:

We all want to know that there is a plan for our lives, especially when we feel lost or uncertain. Anxiety often stems from the fear of the unknown, but God reassures us that he has a plan for each of us — a plan filled with hope and a future. Trusting God's plan means surrendering our need to control and allowing him to guide our steps. His plans are always for our good, even when we don't understand them in the moment.

The voice of self-preservation tells us that no one will protect us as well as we can protect ourselves, so we dare not trust anyone, especially with our future. However, the only way out of the land of mental illness into the land of wholeness and a sound mind is through the valley of surrender to the leading of the Spirit. We have to be able to trust God before we can live in the home and family that he has adopted us into.

I remember being terrified to trust God's Word, because what if it didn't work for me? What if I go off my medication and then have a psychotic break and I spend the rest of my life institutionalized and medicated beyond reality? These were actual thoughts I had. What if I didn't get healed? At least with anxiety and depression I knew what to expect from one day to the next, sort of.

The only way for us to grow in our trust towards our Heavenly Father is to spend time with him. God and his Word are one and the same, so reading his Word is also getting to know his heart. Time in prayer, especially praying in tongues, build us up, and teach us to hear his voice. We have to practice stillness, learning to quiet our minds, and to tune in to the Holy Spirit living inside of us. The One with all the answers is living inside of you. Also, he loves you, a ridiculously lavish amount. Meditate on his love for you.

Can I tell you, falling in love with God is the most exciting experience, and it will change you forever. When you begin to hear his voice on a regular basis, and invite him in to every moment of your day, you'll begin to experience a fullness, and satisfaction like you've never known before.

God's ways are better than you can ever imagine. You will never regret laying it all on the line to trust him with your entire being. You will never regret intimacy with Jesus. Make it a habit. Whatever it takes, commit yourself to trusting God more every day in every area of your life.

Prayer:

Father, I trust Your plan for my life, even when I don't understand it. Help me let go of my need for control and trust that You are working all things for my good, in Jesus' name, Amen.

Challenge:

Think about an area of your life where you've been struggling to trust God's plan. What is the lie that's holding you back? Write it down and I bet you will be surprised by how much less powerful it seems on paper. I dare you, take the leap of faith, surrender that area to him today, and don't look back. I promise you, you will never be the same.

"YOU WILL NEVER REGRET INTIMACY WITH JESUS."

Day 14: Victory Through Christ

Verse: 1 Corinthians 15:57 (CSB)

"But thanks be to God, who gives us the victory through our Lord Jesus Christ!"

Reflection:

We already have victory through Christ, even in the midst of our struggles. Jesus' death and resurrection secured our victory over sin, death, and every form of bondage — including anxiety and depression. Our healing and freedom are part of the victory Jesus won for us on the cross.

We don't fight for victory; we fight from a place of victory. When we remind ourselves of this truth, we can walk in confidence, knowing that Christ has already overcome every obstacle we face, but we still have to stand up and fight to hold on to our victory. Satan and his demonic forces will be trying to dismantle our faith and override our victory in Jesus until the day of His return, but we don't have to give him an inch.

Picture an army that has conquered a great mountain. Their enemies will continually be trying to take the mountain, but as long as they keep watch, a few soldiers can shoot down any climbers, and they can hold on to their victory fairly simply. The more alert they are mentally the less strenuous the fight will be physically.

The same is true of us. The more we are actively aware in the spirit, and are renewing our minds to the word of God, the easier it will be to demolish every attempt of the enemy to derail our thinking, and rob us of our peace.

We don't even have to earn our spot at the top of the mountain. Romans 4:13 tells us that Abraham didn't receive the promise from God because of his ability to follow the law, but rather because his faith in God had qualified him to be called righteous. You only have to believe, that is, have faith that what God says about you, namely that you are righteous, holy, forgiven, and victorious, are true!

You don't have to be perfect for God to see you as perfect. You simply have to believe that he is faithful, trusting that he will do what he said he would do. This faith and trust in him makes you perfect in God's sight.

Prayer:

Thank You, Heavenly Father, for the victory You've given me in Jesus. Help me walk in that victory today, trusting that You've already overcome every battle I face. Help me to see myself the way you see me. In Jesus' name, Amen.

Challenge:

Spend time in worship today, thanking God for the victory he's already given you over anxiety and depression. Write a prayer of thanksgiving for the freedom you have in Christ.

"WE DON'T FIGHT FOR VICTORY; WE FIGHT FROM A PLACE OF VICTORY."

Day 15: Walking in Freedom

Verse: Galatians 5:1 (AMP)

"It was for this freedom that Christ set us free [completely liberating us]; therefore keep standing firm and do not be subject again to a yoke of slavery [which you once removed]."

Reflection:

Jesus didn't just set us free for a moment — he set us free so we can walk in that freedom every day of our lives. However, we must choose to stand firm in that freedom. The enemy will try to pull us back into old patterns of anxiety and depression, but we don't have to let him.

We have the power through Christ to resist those lies and walk in the freedom he's given us. It's not always easy, but it's a daily choice to live in the victory that Jesus won for us.

Yesterday we used the analogy of an army standing firm to maintain the victory over their mountain, but what does that look like practically in our everyday lives?

When I decided to really surrender in obedience and accept God's ways as my ways, it took a lot of unlearning and retraining my mind. In the beginning it was absolutely exhausting as I had a lot of thinking that, I quickly realized, did not line up with the word of God. Every few minutes I was pausing to talk to myself, repeating the truth of God's Word out loud, declaring that I was going to believe the Word instead of the lying thought.

So what do we do?
We have to get into the Word and ask the Holy Spirit to speak to us concerning our situation. We have to speak the Word, out loud, because our brains will more easily accept what they hear our mouths say. We have to repeat the process until God's voice is recognizable, and so is the liars. Then we have to consistently choose to think God's thoughts, and reject the liar's for the rest of our lives, but don't worry, it gets easier, and also kind of hilarious. Who does that liar think he is, really?

The more you practice resisting wrong thinking, and not allowing your emotions or fear to call the shots, the simpler it becomes. The more you immerse yourself in the living Word of God, the more recognizeable that slippery-tongued liar becomes as well.

Prayer:

Lord, help me stand firm in the freedom You've given me. I refuse to go back to the yoke of slavery that once held me captive. Help me walk in Your truth every day, in Jesus' name, Amen.

Challenge:

Think about how you can maintain your freedom in Christ. Write down practical steps that you can take to ensure you're living in the freedom Jesus bought for you, like scheduling daily time without distractions when you can get into the Word, pray in tongues, and be still and listen. Lastly, reflect on what you've learned and what the Holy Spirit has revealed to you over the past fifteen days. Journal it, and be sure to check back on the practical steps you wrote down in order to ensure that you keep walking the walk of freedom.

You are free, my friend, enjoy it!

> "IT'S NOT ALWAYS EASY, BUT IT'S A DAILY CHOICE TO LIVE IN THE VICTORY THAT JESUS WON FOR US."

DON'T MISS "THE GAP"

ABOUT THE AUTHOR

Courtney has been married to her husband Jordan for fourteen years and together they have five children. Courtney has experience in women's and children's ministry through her local church, and she also has an online presence dedicated to helping others find the freedom from mental illness that the Lord revealed to her as a young adult.

FOR MORE FROM THE AUTHOR

Head to her website www.ifcourtneycan.com and follow @ifcourtneycan on Instagram and Facebook.